© 2000 by Barbour Publishing, Inc.

ISBN 1-58660-890-8

Cover image © PhotoDisc, Inc.

All Scripture quotations are from the King James Version of the Bible.

Published by Barbour Publishing, Inc., P. O. Box 719, Uhrichsville, Ohio 44683, www.barbourbooks.com

 Member of the
Evangelical Christian
Publishers Association

Printed in United States of America.
5 4 3 2 1

101 Keys for Life
Powerful Thoughts on Christian Living

Vickie Phelps

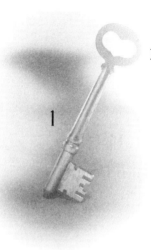

1

No matter what your circumstances,
God's power doesn't change.

With men this is impossible;
but with God all things are possible.

MATTHEW 19:26

———∞∞∞———

2

God doesn't want our spare time,
He wants quality time with us.

And ye shall seek me, and find me,
when ye shall search for me with all your heart.

JEREMIAH 29:13

———∞∞∞———

3

Don't carry grudges—they will never carry you.

Grudge not one against another, brethren,
lest ye be condemned:
behold, the judge standeth before the door.

JAMES 5:9

Use the gifts God has given you instead of
dwelling on the ones He gave someone else.

*And whatsoever ye do in word or deed, do all in
the name of the Lord Jesus, giving thanks to God
and the Father by him.*

COLOSSIANS 3:17

4

∞

Remember, all good gifts are from God.
They're just delivered by people.

*Every good gift and every perfect gift is from above, and
cometh down from the Father of lights.*

JAMES 1:17

5

∞

Don't let the bad habits of others
corrupt your good manners.

Be not deceived: evil communications corrupt good manners.

1 CORINTHIANS 15:33

6

7

Dig a spiritual ditch to retain
some water for the dry spells.

If any man thirst,
let him come unto me, and drink.

JOHN 7:37

8

Believe God's promises. They are without fault.

The Lord is not slack concerning his promise,
as some men count slackness.

2 PETER 3:9

9

Don't be intimidated by what everyone else believes.
Seek to know the truth for yourself.

And ye shall know the truth,
and the truth shall make you free.

JOHN 8:32

If you try to row your own boat,
you may sink it.
Let Jesus row it for you.

I will instruct thee and teach thee
in the way which thou shalt go:
I will guide thee with mine eye.

PSALM 32:8

10

———ᴒᴒᴒ———

Fill the shoes God gave you to wear.
Trying to wear someone else's shoes is painful—
and they never fit right.

But now hath God set the
members every one of them in the body,
as it hath pleased him.

1 CORINTHIANS 12:18

11

12

If God isn't alive in your life,
your words will be dead information.

Set a watch, O LORD, before my mouth;
keep the door of my lips.

PSALM 141:3

⟶⟶⟶⟶

13

God should be CEO of our lives,
not just another board member.

Thou shalt have no other gods before me.

EXODUS 20:3

Forget the past.
You can't build a future by dwelling on history.

Brethren, I count not myself to have apprehended:
but this one thing I do,
forgetting those things which are behind,
and reaching forth unto those things which are before,
I press toward the mark for the prize of
the high calling of God in Christ Jesus.

PHILIPPIANS 3:13–14

1 4

⸺∽∾∿⸺

The reason God doesn't bless some people
with more is that they don't invest wisely.

But lay up for yourselves treasures in heaven,
where neither moth nor rust doth corrupt,
and where thieves do not break through nor steal.

MATTHEW 6:20

15

16

Spend time talking with God every day.

Pray without ceasing.

1 THESSALONIANS 5:17

————

17

Even though God sometimes says "no" to our requests, it's for our own benefit.

Trust in the LORD with all thine heart;
and lean not unto thine own understanding.

PROVERBS 3:5

————

18

Meditate on some portion of your Bible every day.

Thy word have I hid in mine heart,
that I might not sin against thee.

PSALM 119:11

Being a private in God's army is
better than being a general for the devil.

Thou therefore endure hardness,
as a good soldier of Jesus Christ.

2 TIMOTHY 2:3

19

The only way some people will see God is through
your life. Live it accordingly.

Let your light so shine before men,
that they may see your good works,
and glorify your Father which is in heaven.

MATTHEW 5:16

20

Seek out older Christians for advice.

A wise man will hear, and will increase learning;
and a man of understanding shall attain unto wise counsels.

PROVERBS 1:5

21

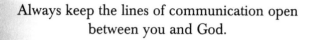

Always keep the lines of communication open
between you and God.

Behold, I stand at the door, and knock:
if any man hear my voice, and open the door,
I will come in to him,
and will sup with him, and he with me.

REVELATION 3:20

⸺◦◦◦⸺

Keep your business deals honest.
That will speak volumes about your character.

Recompense to no man evil for evil.
Provide things honest in the sight of all men.

ROMANS 12:17

Be content with what you have
until God blesses you with more.

For I have learned, in whatsoever state I am,
therewith to be content.

PHILIPPIANS 4:11

24

—∞∞∞—

Be trustworthy.

Lying lips are abomination to the LORD:
but they that deal truly are his delight.

PROVERBS 12:22

25

—∞∞∞—

Attend services at the church of
your choice as often as possible.

Not forsaking the assembling of ourselves together. . .

HEBREWS 10:25

26

It doesn't matter how long something takes—
if it's God's plan, it will happen.

I the LORD have spoken it:
it shall come to pass, and I will do it.

EZEKIEL 24:14

27

———⊸⊸∞⊸———

God doesn't do anything without a reason.
Trust Him.

Commit thy way unto the LORD;
trust also in him;
and he shall bring it to pass.

PSALM 37:5

28

———⊸⊸∞⊸———

Time spent talking to God is never wasted.

Call unto me, and I will answer thee,
and show thee great and mighty things,
which thou knowest not.

JEREMIAH 33:3

29

Take pride in your appearance.
You're God's representative.

That ye would walk worthy of God,
who hath called you unto his kingdom and glory.

1 THESSALONIANS 2:12

30

———⊗⊗⊗———

Half of giving is expecting nothing in return.

Every man according as he purposeth in his heart,
so let him give; not grudgingly, or of necessity:
for God loveth a cheerful giver.

2 CORINTHIANS 9:7

31

———⊗⊗⊗———

Problems should always drive you toward God,
not away from Him.

He shall call upon me, and I will answer him:
I will be with him in trouble;
I will deliver him, and honour him.

PSALM 91:15

32

33

Wounds and scars make a victory sweeter.

I have fought a good fight, I have finished my course,
I have kept the faith:
Henceforth there is laid up for me a crown of righteousness.

2 TIMOTHY 4:7–8

———

34

Take time to listen to someone else's problems.
They may make yours seem smaller.

Bear ye one another's burdens,
and so fulfil the law of Christ.

GALATIANS 6:2

———

35

Be a seed sower instead of a soil inspector.

And that ye study to be quiet, and to do your own business,
and to work with your own hands, as we commanded you.

1 THESSALONIANS 4:11

Be kind to your pets.
They're part of God's creation, too.

A righteous man regardeth the life of his beast:
but the tender mercies of the wicked are cruel.

PROVERBS 12:10

36

Teach your children to pray at an early age.
They will always have a source of strength.

For thou art my hope, O Lord GOD:
thou art my trust from my youth.

PSALM 71:5

37

Family devotions build strong relationships.

Blessed is every one that feareth the LORD;
that walketh in his ways.

PSALM 128:1

38

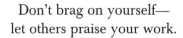

Don't brag on yourself—
let others praise your work.

39

Let another man praise thee, and not thine own mouth;
a stranger, and not thine own lips.

PROVERBS 27:2

—∞∞∞—

Take time to enjoy God's creation.

40

The earth is the LORD'S, and the fulness thereof;
the world, and they that dwell therein.

PSALM 24:1

—∞∞∞—

Don't be so heavenly-minded that
you're of no earthly benefit.

41

That ye might walk worthy of the Lord unto all pleasing,
being fruitful in every good work,
and increasing in the knowledge of God.

COLOSSIANS 1:10

Have a teachable spirit.
You will learn much.

Take fast hold of instruction;
let her not go: keep her; for she is thy life.

PROVERBS 4:13

———⚬⚬⚬———

Don't break another's confidence
in you for any reason.

A talebearer revealeth secrets:
but he that is of a faithful spirit concealeth the matter.

PROVERBS 11:13

———⚬⚬⚬———

Be willing to forgive.
Someday, you may need to be forgiven.

For if ye forgive men their trespasses,
your heavenly Father will also forgive you.

MATTHEW 6:14

Listen to others—
even those younger and less educated.
If God can use a donkey to get a message across,
He can use anyone.

Hear instruction,
and be wise, and refuse it not.

PROVERBS 8:33

⟶⟨ഓ⟩⟵

With God, there are no coincidences.
He always has a plan.

For my thoughts are not your thoughts,
neither are your ways my ways, saith the LORD.

ISAIAH 55:8

45

46

Share your faith with others.

But sanctify the Lord God in your hearts:
and be ready always to give an answer to
every man that asketh you a reason of the hope
that is in you with meekness and fear.

1 PETER 3:15

47

—— ❧ ——

Nothing is too small or too big to pray about.

And this is the confidence that we have in him, that,
if we ask any thing according to his will, he heareth us.

1 JOHN 5:14

48

—— ❧ ——

God will always do what's best for you
if you allow Him to.

Be not ye therefore like unto them:
for your Father knoweth what things ye have need of,
before ye ask him.

MATTHEW 6:8

49

Give God of your time as well as your money.

Seek ye the LORD while he may be found,
call ye upon him while he is near.

ISAIAH 55:6

50

⟨∞⟩

Create a cheerful atmosphere in your home.
It will be a place of refuge from the outside world.

51

The wicked are overthrown, and are not:
but the house of the righteous shall stand.

PROVERBS 12:7

⟨∞⟩

Laugh a lot. It's good medicine.

52

A merry heart doeth good like a medicine:
but a broken spirit drieth the bones.

PROVERBS 17:22

Seek wisdom.
It is a life preserver in the ocean of life.

My son, let not them depart from thine eyes:
keep sound wisdom and discretion.

PROVERBS 3:21

—∞∞—

Write encouraging letters to people
who are feeling down.

A word fitly spoken is like
apples of gold in pictures of silver.

PROVERBS 25:11

—∞∞—

Don't be afraid to say "I'm sorry."

And be ye kind one to another,
tenderhearted, forgiving one another,
even as God for Christ's sake hath forgiven you.

EPHESIANS 4:32

53

54

55

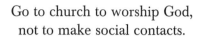

Go to church to worship God,
not to make social contacts.

Enter into his gates with thanksgiving,
and into his courts with praise:
be thankful unto him, and bless his name.

PSALM 100:4

56

God has a plan for you. Seek to know it.

The secret of the LORD is with them that fear him;
and he will show them his covenant.

PSALM 25:14

57

The Lord wants companionship,
so He listens when we talk to Him.

Draw nigh to God,
and he will draw nigh to you.

JAMES 4:8

58

We may not see what God has promised,
but we must trust Him to perform it.

I will cry unto God most high;
unto God that performeth all things for me.

59

PSALM 57:2

———— ⊶∞⊷ ————

God is only as active in our lives
as we allow Him to be.

He that dwelleth in the secret place
of the most High shall abide
under the shadow of the Almighty.

60

PSALM 91:1

———— ⊶∞⊷ ————

Lighten your load before your ship is wrecked.

Come unto me, all ye that labour and are heavy laden,
and I will give you rest.

61

MATTHEW 11:28

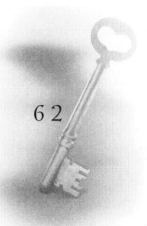

62

Satan is the stress-maker,
but Jesus is the stress-breaker.

Thou wilt keep him in perfect peace,
whose mind is stayed on thee:
because he trusteth in thee.

ISAIAH 26:3

63

If you want more from your church,
try putting more into it.

For we are labourers together with God:
ye are God's husbandry, ye are God's building.

1 CORINTHIANS 3:9

64

Never let social status influence
your relationship with God.

That your faith should not stand in the wisdom of men,
but in the power of God.

1 CORINTHIANS 2:5

God has given you gifts and
abilities that only you can use.

As every man hath received the gift,
even so minister the same one to another,
as good stewards of the manifold grace of God.

1 PETER 4:10

65

God places people in strategic places
to carry out His plans.
Where are you?

And who knoweth whether thou art come to
the kingdom for such a time as this?

ESTHER 4:14

66

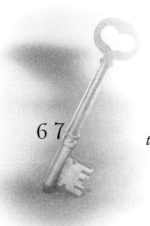

Obey God's speed limit.
Don't get ahead of Him.

But they that wait upon the LORD
shall renew their strength;
they shall mount up with wings as eagles;
they shall run, and not be weary;
and they shall walk, and not faint.

ISAIAH 40:31

67

If you don't give up, God won't give up.

What shall we then say to these things?
If God be for us, who can be against us?

ROMANS 8:31

68

Prayer is the Christian's most effective weapon.

The effectual fervent prayer of
a righteous man availeth much.

JAMES 5:16

69

Don't speak rashly.
Bitter words make a poor meal.

He that keepeth his mouth keepeth his life: but he that
openeth wide his lips shall have destruction.

PROVERBS 13:3

70

There's a time for everything—God's time.

To every thing there is a season,
and a time to every purpose under the heaven.

ECCLESIASTES 3:1

71

When life gets the darkest,
remember Jesus is the Light.

Then spake Jesus again unto them, saying,
I am the light of the world:
he that followeth me shall not walk in darkness,
but shall have the light of life.

JOHN 8:12

72

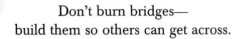

Don't burn bridges—
build them so others can get across.

Withhold not good from them to whom it is due,
when it is in the power of thine hand to do it.

PROVERBS 3:27

———✺———

Don't concentrate on your problems.
Concentrate on Christ.

I can do all things through Christ
which strengtheneth me.

PHILIPPIANS 4:13

———✺———

Make time for worship—
it's the oasis in your desert.

He maketh me to lie down in green pastures:
he leadeth me beside the still waters.

PSALM 23:2

Christians should grow and produce fruit,
not get overripe on the vine.

I am the vine, ye are the branches:
He that abideth in me, and I in him,
the same bringeth forth much fruit:
for without me ye can do nothing.

JOHN 15:5

76

———∞———

Don't just roll with the flow.
The river may be flowing in the wrong direction.

Wherefore, my beloved,
as ye have always obeyed,
not as in my presence only,
but now much more in my absence,
work out your own salvation with fear and trembling.

PHILIPPIANS 2:12

77

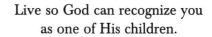

Live so God can recognize you
as one of His children.

*For as many as are led by the Spirit of God,
they are the sons of God.*

ROMANS 8:14

※

Go toward God—
He'll meet you halfway.

*All that the Father giveth me shall come to me;
and him that cometh to me I will in no wise cast out.*

JOHN 6:37

※

People who never get out of the boat
can't expect to walk on water.

*For God hath not given us the spirit of fear;
but of power, and of love, and of a sound mind.*

2 TIMOTHY 1:7

78

79

80

Anything God gives you is worth holding on to.

Blessed be the Lord,
who daily loadeth us with benefits,
even the God of our salvation.

PSALM 68:19

8 1

When you let go of God's hand,
you're on your own.

It is God that girdeth me with strength,
and maketh my way perfect.

PSALM 18:32

82

If you don't stand for God,
you'll fall for everything.

Watch ye, stand fast in the faith,
quit you like men, be strong.

1 CORINTHIANS 16:13

83

You can't turn over a new leaf
if the tree is dead.

Therefore if any man be in Christ,
he is a new creature:
old things are passed away;
behold, all things are become new.

2 CORINTHIANS 5:17

—⟨∞⟩—

84

God doesn't have accidents or make mistakes.
He knows what He's doing.

Be strong and of a good courage,
fear not, nor be afraid of them:
for the LORD thy God,
he it is that doth go with thee;
he will not fail thee, nor forsake thee.

DEUTERONOMY 31:6

85

Happiness is an inside job that
shows up on the outside.

Happy is that people, whose God is the LORD.

PSALM 144:15

———✤———

Everybody in God's army is a volunteer.
We serve God out of love.

We love him, because he first loved us.

1 JOHN 4:19

———✤———

Prayer is preventative medicine
for life's problems.

Casting all your care upon him;
for he careth for you.

1 PETER 5:7

86

87

88

89

You don't need a big storm to destroy you.
A little wind or water in your life
can do a lot of damage.

*God is our refuge and strength,
a very present help in trouble.*

PSALM 46:1

━━○○○━━

90

We need to get on God's schedule
instead of trying to fit Him into ours.

Be still, and know that I am God.

PSALM 46:10

━━○○○━━

91

Keeping God first in your life
should be your top priority.

*But seek ye first the kingdom of God,
and his righteousness;
and all these things shall be added unto you.*

MATTHEW 6:33

God accepts us as we are,
but He would like to see some improvement
along the way.

Blessed is the man whom thou chastenest,
O LORD, and teachest him out of thy law.

PSALM 94:12

92

———⌾———

God will not give us a job to do
without qualifying and equipping us
to do the work.

If a man therefore purge himself from these,
he shall be a vessel unto honour, sanctified,
and meet for the master's use,
and prepared unto every good work.

2 TIMOTHY 2:21

93

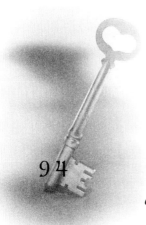

God's plan will be fulfilled
whether we're a part of it or not—
but it's a wonderful feeling
to find our place in the plan.

Therefore, my beloved brethren,
be ye stedfast, unmoveable,
always abounding in the work of the Lord,
forasmuch as ye know that your labour
is not in vain in the Lord.

1 CORINTHIANS 15:58

❦

If we plant the right kind of seeds,
we'll harvest the right crop in our lives.

For he that soweth to his flesh
shall of the flesh reap corruption;
but he that soweth to the Spirit
shall of the Spirit reap life everlasting.

GALATIANS 6:8

95

If you want to be the salt of the earth, you have to be
willing to be shaken out of the box.

Ye are the salt of the earth: but if the salt have lost his
savour, wherewith shall it be salted?

MATTHEW 5:13

96

————

If you want to carry on a conversation with God,
you must also be a willing listener.

Incline your ear, and come unto me:
hear, and your soul shall live;
and I will make an everlasting covenant with you.

ISAIAH 55:3

97

————

God doesn't want to hear excuses,
He wants to see action.

But be ye doers of the word, and not hearers only,
deceiving your own selves.

JAMES 1:22

98

99

When the going gets tough, the wise go to Jesus.

Let us therefore come boldly unto the throne of grace,
that we may obtain mercy,
and find grace to help in time of need.

HEBREWS 4:16

———◦◦◦———

100

It is not what we can do that counts,
but what God can do through us.

Not that we are sufficient of ourselves
to think any thing as of ourselves;
but our sufficiency is of God.

2 CORINTHIANS 3:5

———◦◦◦———

101

God never leaves us.
We're the ones who move.

For he hath said, I will never leave thee,
nor forsake thee.

HEBREWS 13:5